# Flying Fiddle Duets

## for two violas

Book One                                    Myanna Harvey

### CHP268

Cover painting by Gregory El Harvey
For more information, visit www.gregharveygallery.com

# Flying Fiddle Duets for Two Violas

Traditional Tunes, arranged by Myanna Harvey

## Table of Contents

| Title | Page |
|---|---|
| 1. John Ryan's Polka | 2 |
| 2. The Irish Washerwoman | 4 |
| 3. Swallowtail Jig | 6 |
| 4. Johnny's Gone for a Soldier | 7 |
| 5. Drunken Sailor | 8 |
| 6. Greensleeves | 10 |
| 7. Soldier's Joy | 12 |
| 8. Star of the County Down | 14 |
| 9. The Water is Wide | 15 |
| 10. Lannigan's Ball | 16 |
| 11. 1812 Quickstep | 18 |
| 12. Shenandoah | 20 |
| 13. All the Pretty Horses | 22 |
| 14. Fire in the Mountain | 24 |
| 15. Devil Among the Tailors | 26 |
| 16. Liberty | 28 |
| 17. The Girl I Left Behind Me | 30 |
| 18. Ballad of the Green Mountain Boys | 32 |
| 19. St. Patrick's Day | 34 |

# Flying Fiddle Duets for Two Violas, Book One

## John Ryan's Polka

Trad., arr. Myanna Harvey

# The Irish Washerwoman

Trad., arr. M. Harvey

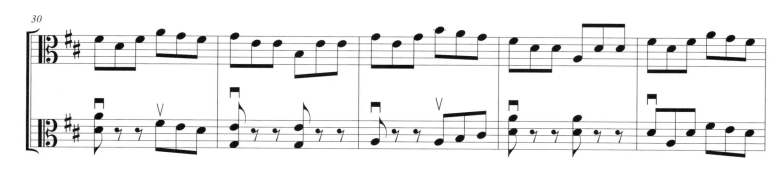

# Swallowtail Jig

Trad., arr. M. Harvey

# Johnny's Gone for a Soldier

Trad., arr. M. Harvey

# Drunken Sailor

Trad., arr. M. Harvey

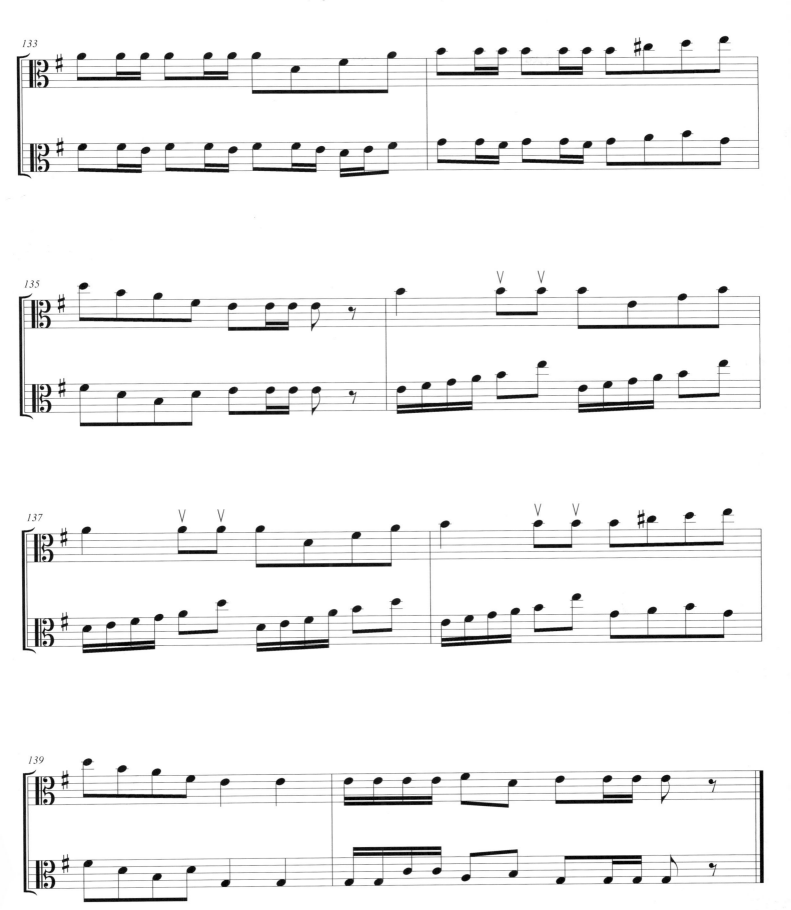

# Greensleeves

Trad., arr. M. Harvey

rit.

12

# Soldier's Joy

Trad., arr. M. Harvey

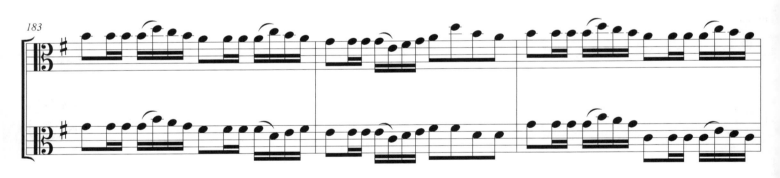

# Star of the County Down

Trad., arr. M. Harvey

# The Water is Wide

Trad., arr. M. Harvey

# Lannigan's Ball

Trad., arr. M. Harvey

# 1812 Quickstep

Trad., arr. M. Harvey

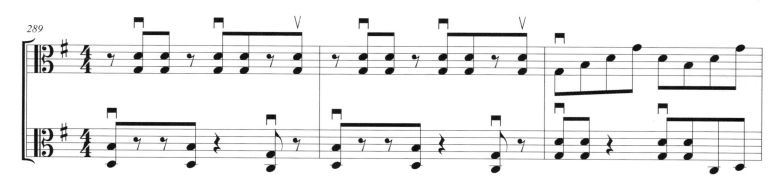

# Shenandoah

Trad., arr. M. Harvey

# All the Pretty Horses

Trad., arr. M. Harvey

This Page Left Blank
to Eliminate Page Turns

# Fire in the Mountain

Trad., arr. M. Harvey

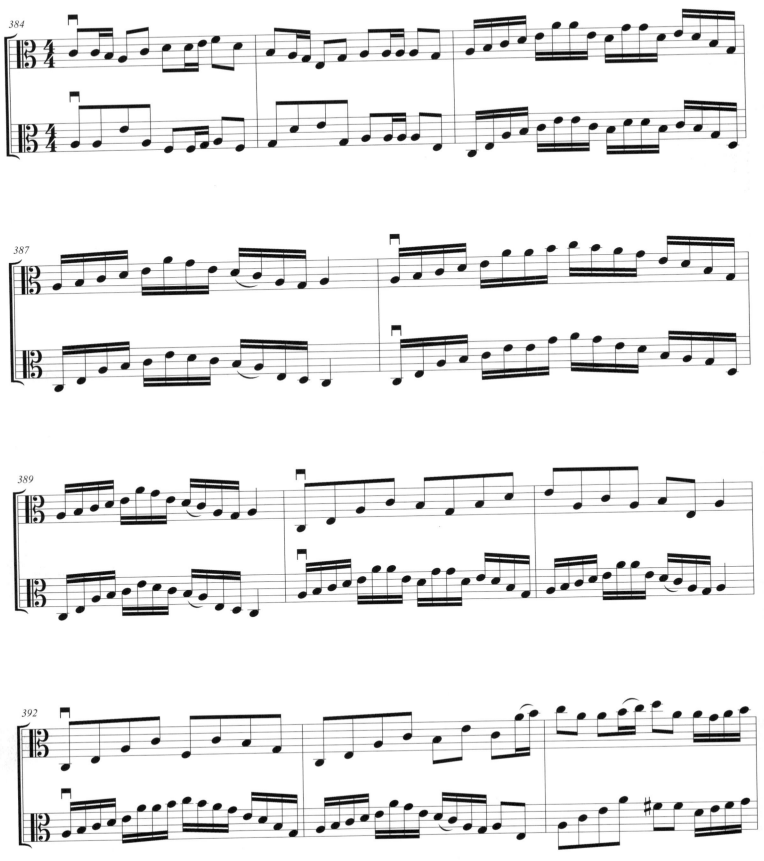

# Devil Among the Tailors

Trad., arr. M. Harvey

# Liberty

Trad., arr. M. Harvey

# The Girl I Left Behind Me

Trad., arr. M. Harvey

# Ballad of the Green Mountain Boys

Trad., arr. M. Harvey

# St. Patrick's Day

Trad., arr. M. Harvey

The Triplet Book for Viola, Part One

Cassia Harvey

Left-Hand Warm-Up: G Major

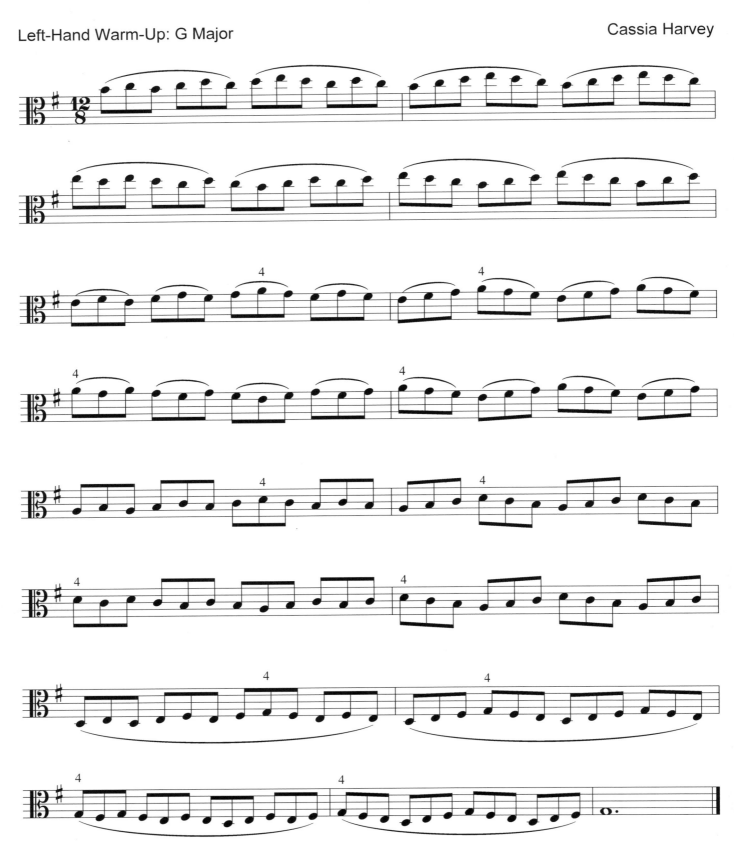

Made in the USA
Middletown, DE
07 March 2015